# HANDS-ON
# design

**Ivan Bulloch**
**Tony Chambers**

Author: Diane James
Photography: Toby Maudsley
Cover Photography: James Johnson

TWO-CAN

# Contents

# 4 Equipment

Here are some of the things that will be useful when embarking on a design project. Most of them can be bought from art or stationery shops.

Try to keep all of your
equipment as clean as
possible and make sure
that you have a clear
surface to work on!

# 6 Using Equipment

▶ Use a roller to spread paint smoothly over printing blocks. You can use a clean roller to smooth over surfaces.

▶ Felt-tip pens come in different thicknesses. Thick pens are good for filling in areas of colour and thin ones for outlining.

▲ Look for 'safety'
craft knives with
retractable blades.

▲ Trace letters from magazines
and newspapers. Transfer the trace
to stencil card and cut the shape
out. Use a stencil brush with short,
hard bristles to apply the paint.

# 8 Letters

The use of letters is called *typography*. Letters can be formed in hundreds of different ways. Different styles of letters are known as *typefaces* and different typefaces have special names such as Baskerville, Bodoni, Times and Frankfurter! Most typefaces in regular use were designed many years ago but new ones are still being created. The typeface you are reading now is called Helvetica.

Letters within a particular typeface can vary enormously. They can be large or small and they can be made tall and thin or short and fat.

Some letters have curved, wedge-like endings. These are called *serifs*. Letters without serifs are known as *sans serif*.

## Collecting letters

To find out more about letters, make a collection of as many different typefaces as you can find from magazines, newspapers and packages.

# 10 Making Letters

Once you have a grasp of existing letter forms, it's time to experiment with your own versions! A wide variety of equipment and techniques can be used to produce letters. You can use paint, ink, coloured pencils, torn or cut paper or card, shaped balsa wood, wooden blocks, pre-formed sticky shapes or stencils. Different techniques can be combined to produce interesting effects.

Depending on the materials you choose, letters can be free and flowing – such as the brush stroke 'S' here, or rigid and solid like the letters made from children's building blocks.

The examples on these pages show how letters can be made from the simplest of shapes. In most cases, simpler letter forms lead to easier reading!

The letters 'P,E,A' at the bottom right are made by cutting and tearing coloured paper to the inner and outer shapes of letters – in other words, making letters in reverse.

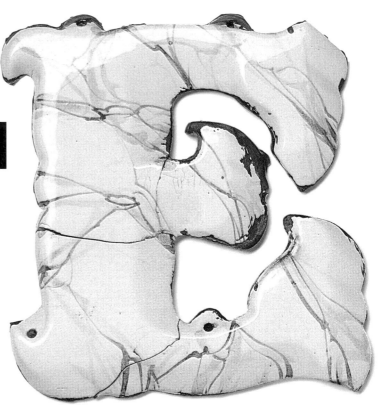

## 12 **Raised Letters**

Most of the type we are surrounded by comes in printed form – newspapers, magazines, posters and packaging – but not all letters are flat!

The letters on these pages are made from plastic, wood and metal. The letter 'S' painted on glass is flat but given dimension by clever shading.

Raised letters can be bold and simple or very ornate. Look at shop signs, cinema and theatre fronts and old buildings. It is well worth keeping a camera or sketch book with you to record interesting examples of raised letters.

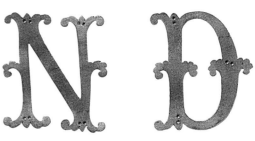

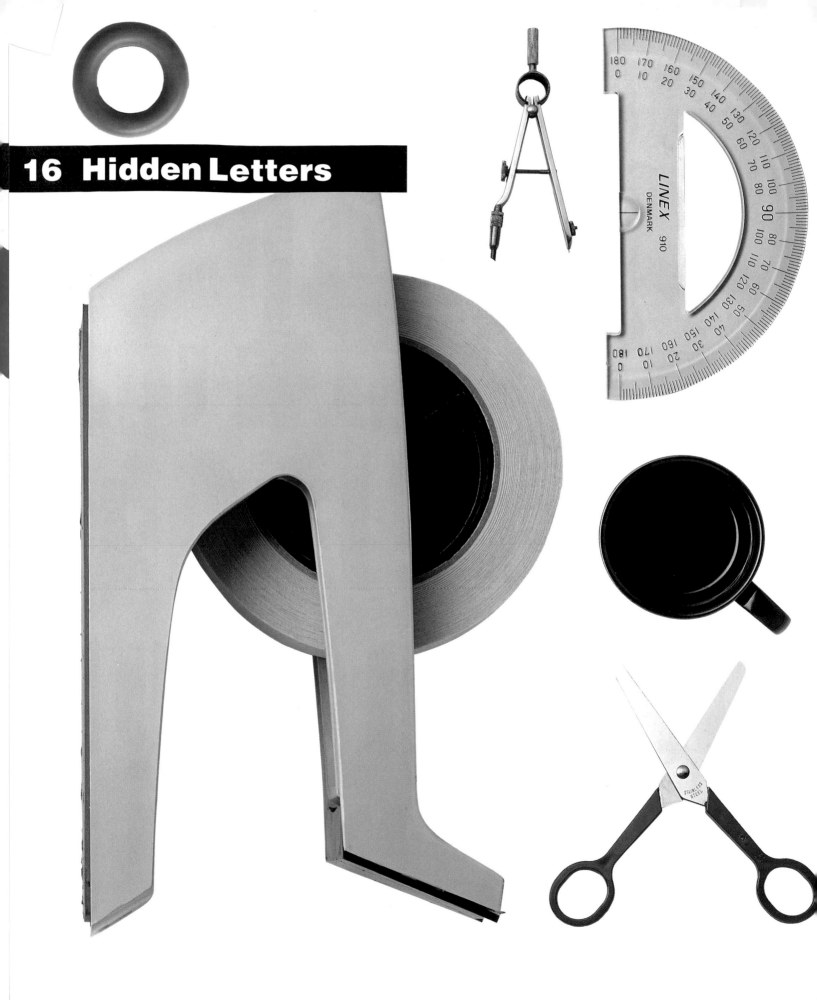

Letter forms can be found in the most unlikely places as you will see from the objects on this page! A tape dispenser on its side becomes an interesting 'R', a bendy straw an 'L' and a razor an elegant 'T'.

How many letters can you see by just looking around you? Try making up a complete alphabet from objects.

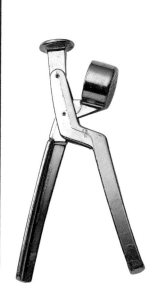

# 18 Badges

Once you have made one badge you won't be able to stop! First, sketch a page of rough designs. Choose the ones you like best and work the designs out in detail. Badges do not have to be round so try experimenting with different shapes.

Some badges carry a message or advertise a product, others are worn just for fun.

Most of the badges here were made by sticking paper shapes onto card but you could also use paint or felt-tip pens.

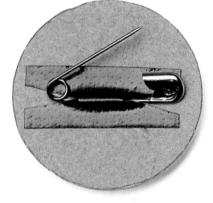

▲ Cut a piece of strong tape to fit on the back of the badge. Make notches in the ends of the tape and stick it firmly over a safety pin.

# 20 Letterheads

Printed stationery is expensive to produce but it is not difficult to make your own! Choose a method that can be easily repeated so that you can make a good supply. Here are some ideas using stencils, rubber stamps and a simple printing set bought from a stationery shop.

Having decided whether you want to produce cards, writing paper or envelopes – or a combination – it is worth spending some time on rough designs. Decide how many colours you want to use and keep the design as simple as possible.

▼ *When you cut a stencil, keep the inner letters. You can position these on your paper and spray over them for a reverse effect.*

▲ *This stamp of a rubber 5 and the letters LA were cut from ordinary rubbers. Remember to cut the figures or letters in reverse so that they will be the right way round when printed.*

5 2 KNOWSLEY ROAD SW11

Jean,
Paris

...Y ROAD S...

A

# 22 Pop-up Letters

By cutting and scoring on concertina folds you can make letters that stand up on their own! Experiment with your initials and when you have perfected the technique, try making some stationery like the examples here.

▲ *This is part of a complete pop-up alphabet made by artist/designer Ron King. Try making your own!*

# 24 Packaging I

Have you noticed how many of the things you buy have printed packaging? The aim of the packaging is to give you an idea of what is inside and to make you want to pick the product up.

Packaging design combines type, symbols and sometimes illustrations or photographs – colour is also very important.

The designer must bear in mind who is most likely to want the product and design the packaging for that market.

Some packaging, such as the Coca-Cola can here, has changed very little over the years. Other packaging designs change frequently to suit the fashion of the day.

Build up your own collection of packaging, looking particularly for well-designed examples that put their message across strongly.

▲ Cut a shape in a matchbox and cover with paper.

▼ Cover the lid of an existing box with paper and stick on paper shapes.

▲ Make your own cassette covers by putting together an appropriate collage.

▼ Use spray paint or a splattering technique over objects such as nuts and bolts.

Find an existing package that is the right size for your 'product'. Open it out carefully and put it on a piece of card. Draw round the edges to make a pattern. Score along fold lines and assemble your package. Try different techniques for decorating your packages.

## 28 Carrier Bags I

Many shops use carrier bags as a form of advertising. If the design of the bag is successful, people are more likely to remember the shop and go there again!

It is important that the design reflects the product that the shop sells and appeals to its customers.

Decorate bags with spray paint and stencils or paper collage. Remember that you can use both parts of cut stencils – the bits cut out of the stencil card and the shapes left behind. This will give you either a positive or negative image. You can also use card shapes to mask out areas when spraying.

Look carefully at how existing carrier bags are made and use them as patterns for making your own. Handles can be made from folded paper stuck firmly to the inside of the bag or cord slotted through holes. Use stiff paper to make your bags and don't overload them!

Posters are used for passing on information and it is important that they are as eye-catching as possible. Strong typography is important.

All of the posters here were made using techniques from this book. You may want to make more than one poster. Using stencils and masking off areas with card makes the process much quicker. Think about how the images and type should work together to put across a strong message.

# 38 Colour II

If you look at any of the colour pictures in this book through a magnifying glass you will see that they have been made up of dots. The picture on the right shows this more clearly. The dots are larger and closer together in the dark areas and smaller and wider apart in the light areas.

Before a colour illustration can be printed using the four-colour process it must be separated into four blocks.

The Bridgeman Art Library

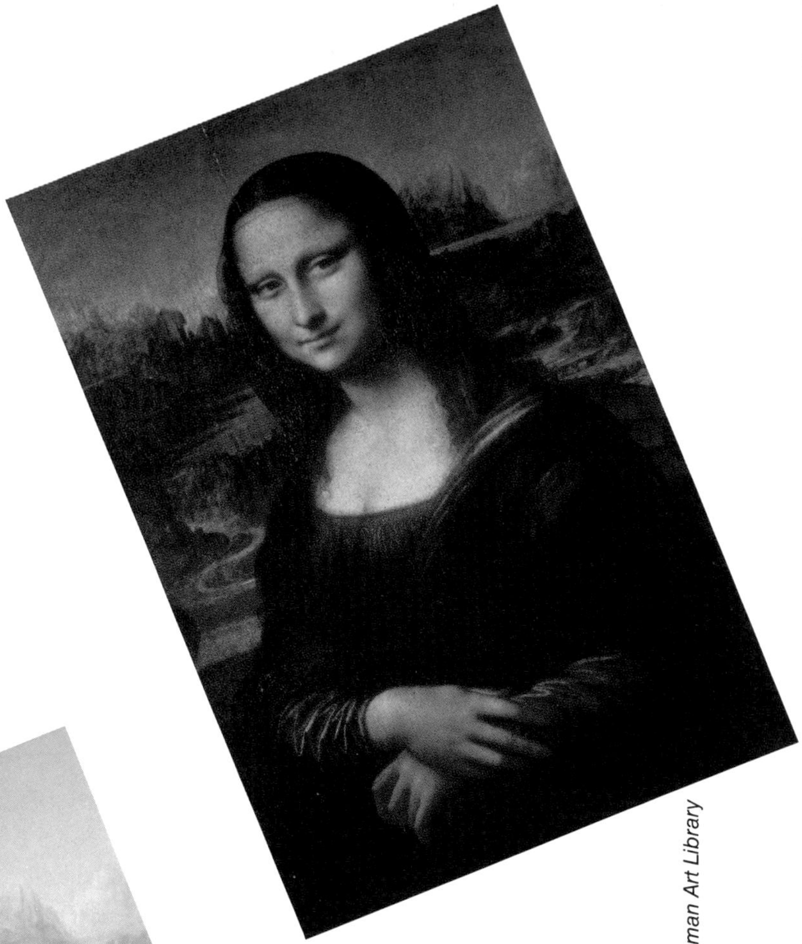

*When these four blocks are printed together the result is the picture at the top.*

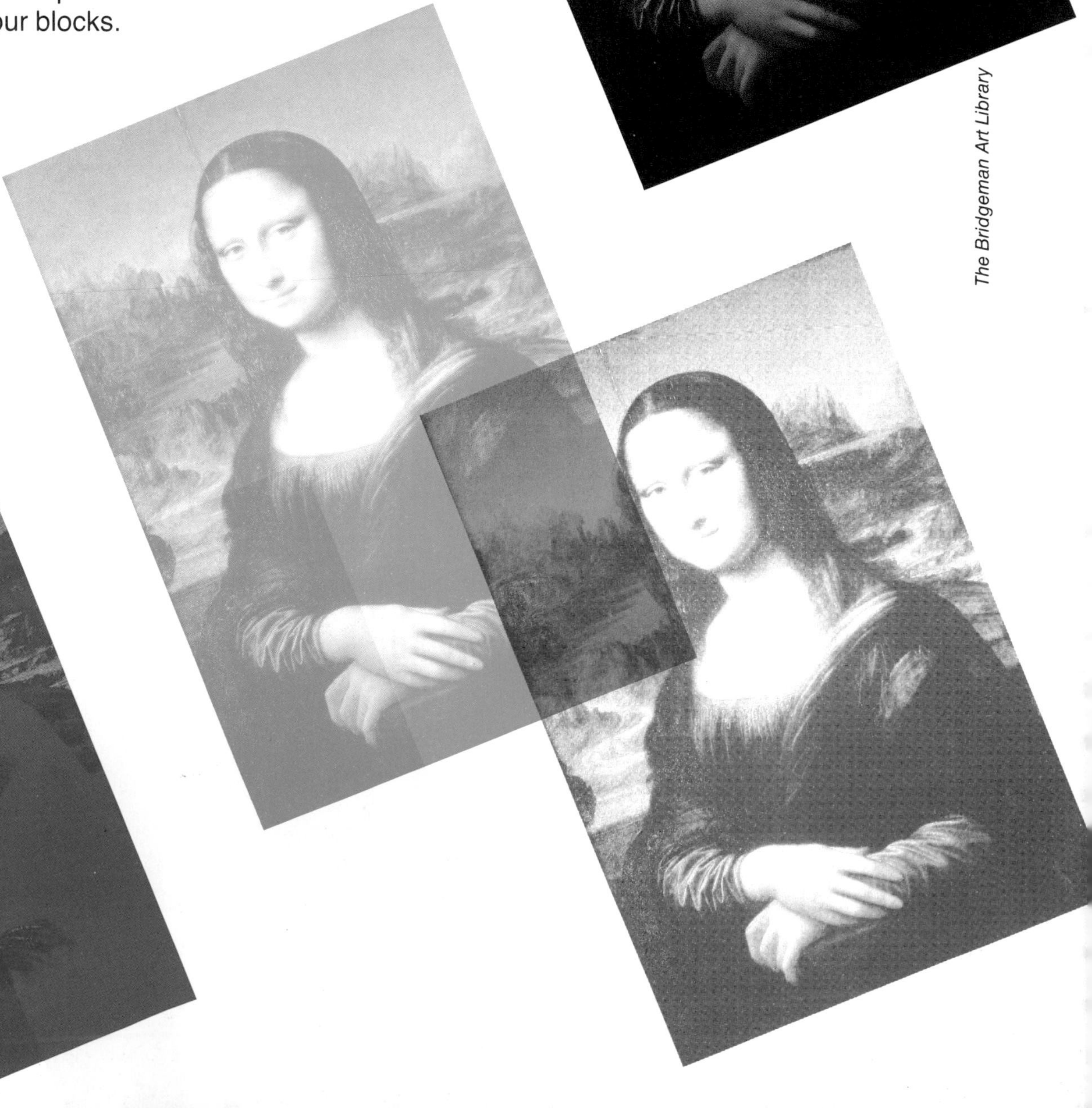

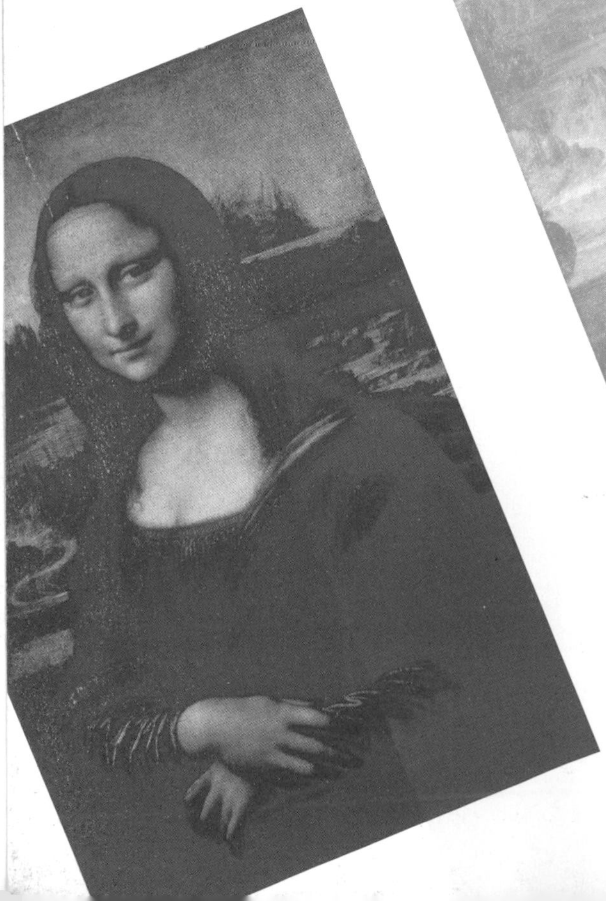

Nearly all the pages in magazines, books and newspapers are designed using a printed 'grid' like the one here. The grid imposes certain rules such as length of type and width of margins.

All of the elements here are being used to create a layout on the theme 'faces'. Some of the faces have been made as models. These must be photographed. Others are illustrations and do not need to be photographed.

Try designing your own layout using photographs, drawings and either hand or type-written text.

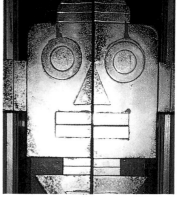

Here you can see how the elements on the previous pages have been organised to give a balanced page layout. The designer has used a simple four column grid. Some of the pictures take up one column and some two.

If you look through the pages in this book you will see that certain rules have been followed. The main headings are always in the same place and the type is the same size throughout. However, rules can be broken if the designer feels that the result will be more interesting.

Look through a selection of magazines and newspapers and see if you can work out what sort of grid the designer has used. How many different typefaces have been used? Which pages stand out and why?

Try drawing your own grids. Experiment with different size margins at the sides and top and bottom. Cut out type and pictures from a magazine and place them on your grid. Try to get a good balance between type and pictures.

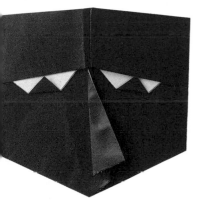

## 44 Scrapbook

It is hard to sit in front of a blank sheet of paper when tackling a design problem. Some sort of inspiration is often needed! Try building up a collection of things that you like or admire. This might include postcards, photographs, stamps, magazines, packaging, sketches, labels and anything else that catches your eye.

## 46 Brainstorming I

Brainstorming means thinking very hard about a particular project and coming up with a number of solutions before reaching the final design.

   This project is to make an illustration from letters, punctuation marks and numbers. You could extend the project to illustrating a book in this way.

# INDEX

Design copyright © Ivan Bulloch and Tony Chambers, 1990
Text and compilation copyright © Two-Can Publishing Ltd, 1990

First published in Great Britain in 1990 by
Two-Can Publishing Ltd, 27 Cowper Street, London EC2A 4AP

Printed in Great Britain

British Library Cataloguing in Publication Data
Bulloch, Ivan
Design
    1. Graphic design. Techniques.
    I. Title
    741.6

    ISBN 1-85434-009-3

CREDITS
p.12 Raised letters lent by Nicholas Biddulph: Central Lettering Library
p.42 Typographical 'faces' by Grundy & Northedge
p.46 Inspired by El Lissitsky